Perfectly You

published by

National Center for Youth Issues

Practical Guidance Resources
Educators Can Trust

ncyi.org

www.ncyi.org

For practical resources including
websites, suggested reading material, games,
and interactive lesson plans, please visit
www.ncyi.org/perfectlyyou

Duplication and Copyright

National Center for Youth Issues
Practical Guidance Resources
Educators Can Trust

P.O. Box 22185
Chattanooga, TN 37422-2185
423.899.5714 • 800.477.8277
fax: 423.899.4547
www.ncyi.org

ISBN: 978-1-931636-88-9
© 2009 National Center for Youth Issues, Chattanooga, TN
All rights reserved.

Written by: Julia V. Taylor
Illustrations by: Phillip W. Rodgers
Published by National Center for Youth Issues
Hardcover

Printed in Mexico

Thanks to my perfectly unique family and friends;

I love you all.

–Julia

There is nobody in the world exactly like you.

You're one of a kind, and that's sort of cool!

Be delighted to be just who you are.

Accept yourself – because you're a STAR!

You only get one body, so love what you've got.

Don't waste your time wishing you're someone you're not.

Because all bodies are different!

Imagine what it would be like – if we all looked the same?

What a plain, boring sight!

You're spectacular and silly, gracious and kind.

You've got a great heart and you've got a great mind.

Put them to use - you can start right now!

No more excuses, I'll teach you how.

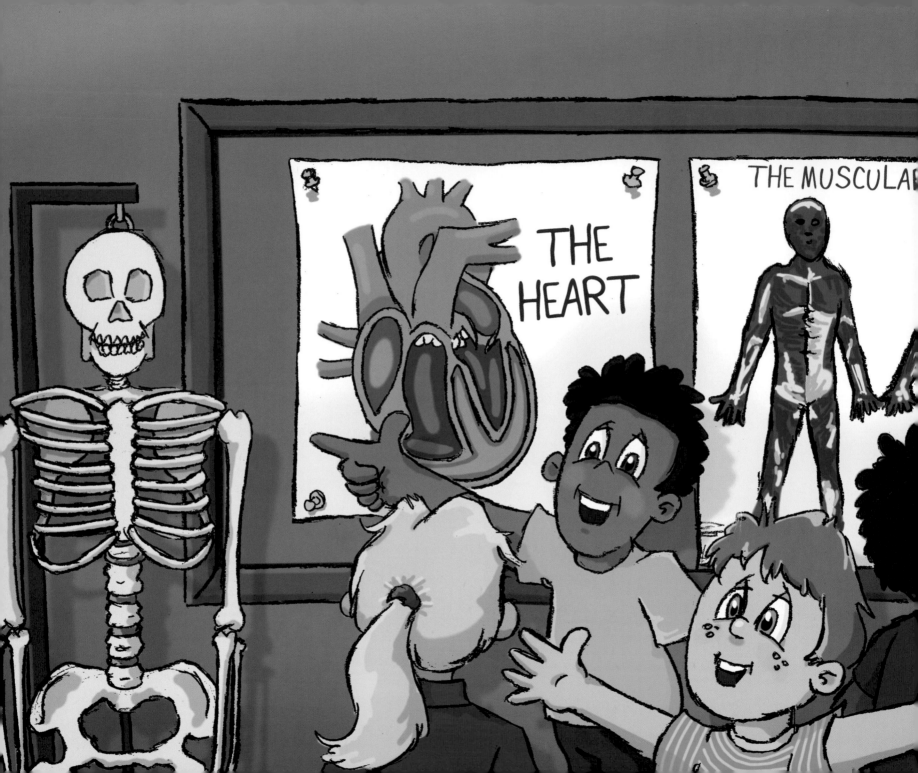

EAT HEALTHY FOODS

Eat breakfast every morning,

it's the most important meal!

It gives you energy, wakes you up,

and you'll like how you feel!

Have some fruits and veggies,

and eat lots of whole grains,

And don't forget the milk,

it's even good plain!

MOVE YOUR BODY

Make sure you exercise, get out and go play.

Try to keep yourself moving, every single day.

Anyone can exercise, it's easy – and fun!

You can jump rope, swim, ride a bike, or run!

GO FOR IT

Try new things, so that you will know
if you like them or not - don't go with the flow!
Do what makes you happy - there is only one you!
So do what you love, and love what you do!

BE POSITIVE

Look on the bright side and think happy thoughts.
Because no body's perfect, every body has faults.

In case you doubt yourself and
don't think it's true,
remind yourself —
"I'm ridiculously cool!"

TALK ABOUT IT

Show your feelings, don't hold them inside.

You can be mad, sad, or glad – and you can even cry.

It's normal to have feelings, and not all of them are good.

Talk about them with an adult, and feel what you should.

YOU CAN DO IT

Believe in yourself. Be confident and true!

You are spectacular! You are you!

You have special talents. Some that no one else can do!

SPREAD SUNSHINE

Be kind to others and they'll be kind to you.

You get what you give – I know this to be true.

So show your smile often and try to get along

to make the world happy, to make the world strong!

Stay Strong

Take care of your body, through good times and bad

And make every day the best you've ever had!

Trust yourself and what you stand for,

Because you're "perfectly you", and you're ready to soar!